Author:
John Malam studied ancient history and archaeology at the University of Birmingham. He then worked as an archaeologist at the Ironbridge Gorge Museum, Shropshire. He is now an author, specializing in non-fiction books for children. He lives in Cheshire with his wife and their two children.

Artist:
David Antram was born in Brighton, England, in 1958. He studied at Eastbourne College of Art and then worked in advertising for fifteen years before becoming a full-time artist. He has illustrated many children's non-fiction books.

Series Creator:
David Salariya was born in Dundee, Scotland. He has illustrated a wide range of books and has created and designed many new series for publishers both in the U.K. and overseas. In 1989, he established The Salariya Book Company. He lives in Brighton with his wife, illustrator Shirley Willis, and their son Jonathan.

Editors:
Karen Barker Smith
Stephanie Cole

Created, design and produced by
The Salariya Book Company Ltd
Book House, 25 Marlborough Place,
Brighton BN1 1UB

Visit The Salariya Book Company at:
www.salariya.com
www.book-house.co.uk

ISBN 0-531-14607-3 (Lib. Bdg.)
ISBN 0-531-16368-7 (Pbk.)

Published in the United States by Franklin Watts
A Division of Scholastic Inc.
90 Sherman Turnpike, Danbury, CT 06816

A CIP catalog record for this title is available from the Library of Congress.

Printed and bound in Belgium.

Printed on paper from sustainable forests.

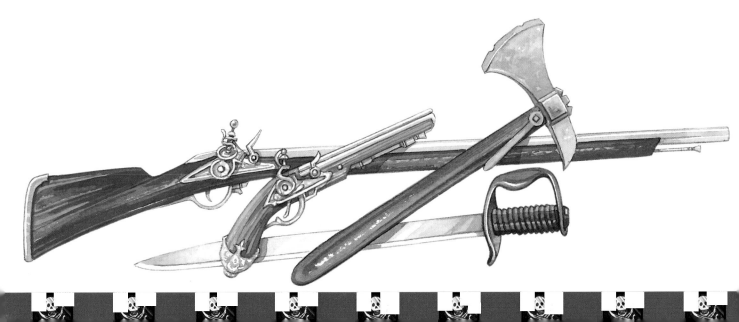

You Wouldn't Want to Be a Pirate's Prisoner!

How did I get into this mess?!

Horrible Things You'd Rather Not Know

Written by
John Malam

Illustrated by
David Antram

Created and designed by
David Salariya

W
FRANKLIN WATTS
A Division of Scholastic Inc.
NEW YORK • TORONTO • LONDON • AUCKLAND • SYDNEY
MEXICO CITY • NEW DELHI • HONG KONG
DANBURY, CONNECTICUT

Contents

Introduction

It is 1716, and the Caribbean Sea is the haunt of English pirates. These rogues are the menace of the Spanish Main. This is the area of land and sea between the northern coast of South America and the southern shores of North America. Pirates like to lie in wait for Spanish treasure ships laden with gold and jewels from the peoples of the New World.

You are the captain of one of these ships. You hope to sail home safely to Spain, unseen by the scoundrels that lurk in these dangerous waters. To the pirates, your golden galleon is a great prize. If they capture it, you wouldn't want to become a pirate's prisoner!

Treasure Fleet! Your Ship Sets Sail

In Your Ship's Hold:

GOLD AND RICHES. At the port of Cartagena, you collected gold, emeralds, pearls, and valuable timber from the rain forests of South America.

You are the captain of a Spanish galleon. It is a large, slow-moving ship armed with cannons and a hold full of precious cargo. Once a year you sail home to Spain from a port in the Spanish Main. It would be foolish to set sail on your own, so you sail in a convoy with many other galleons. There is safety in numbers. If a pirate attacks the fleet, he will probably pick on one ship at a time. You hope it will not be yours!

VERA CRUZ. At this port, you stopped for porcelain, silk, and spices from lands across the Pacific Ocean.

SPANISH CAPTAIN. Dressed in your captain's clothes, you are a grand sight. Your crew respects you, and you are proud that your ship has never been attacked by pirates.

We are shipshape and ready to go!

SUPPLIES. At Havana you bought copper, food, and water for the long voyage home.

Handy Hint

Sail close to the warship that sails with the fleet. It is there to protect you.

NORTH AMERICA

BAHAMAS

Vera Cruz

Havana

CUBA

CENTRAL AMERICA

JAMAICA

Caribbean Sea

HISPANIOLA

Cartagena

SOUTH AMERICA

WEST INDIES

N

W

E

S

THE FLEET. In the 1600s, Spanish treasure fleets sailed with as many as ninety galleons. Now, in the early 1700s, the fleet has fewer than twelve ships.

Map of the Spanish Main in the 18th century

Pirates, Wolves of the Sea

From Privateer to Pirate

Privateers were English, French, and Dutch men who had permission from their governments to attack Spanish ships and territory in the New World. That has come to an end, but some privateers are still up to their old tricks. They steal for themselves as pirates.

After

Before

English pirates have been attacking Spanish treasure fleets for almost two hundred years. Sometimes they raid ships while they are at anchor in port. Other times they take to the open sea and look for a ship that has fallen behind the rest of the fleet. The first twenty years of the 18th century have been a good time for piracy in the Spanish Main. There are more pirates here than ever before. They have turned many island ports into their own safe havens.

NO MORE WAR. England and Holland were at war against France and Spain until 1714. Many sea captains fought as privateers and raided Spanish ships. The end of the war has put them out of a job, so they have turned to piracy.

Treasure ships ahoy, Cap'n!

PIRATE HAVEN. The island of New Providence offers safety to pirate ships and their crews. It is a wild, lawless place where hundreds of pirates are based.

9

Pirate's Prize

Avast! Here Be Pirates!

THE PIRATE SHIP. It is a sloop, a small, lightweight vessel that cuts quickly through the water. It is perfect for surprise attacks.

PIRATE FLAG. The Jolly Roger is black with a white human skull. It is designed to strike fear into your heart.

Your ship has set sail with six others, all bound for Spain. Your galleon is so weighed down with loot that it cannot keep up with the fleet. You fall behind and are on your own, with no one to come to your aid if something happens.

A ship has been following the fleet at a distance, and it closes in on you. The ship raises its flag to identify itself. Only then do you know you are about to be attacked by pirates! The smaller, faster ship quickly reaches your galleon. Soon the English pirates are boarding your vessel to relieve you of its treasure.

CAPTAIN. He is an outlaw who is known for getting exactly what he wants.

WEAPONS. They might be dressed in rags, but pirates are armed with a fearsome range of weapons.

Boarding ax

Flintlock pistol

Cutlass

Musket

Captured!

The pirate captain is not satisfied with the loot from your ship. He wants the treasure from the rest of the fleet, too. That is why he needs you. Now you are the pirate's prisoner, and you are at his mercy. He wants you to tell him what course the other treasure ships are taking. It's no use saying you don't know, because these ruffians know you do. They have ways of making you talk!

So where be your fleet, then?

Rules of Piracy

BOOTY. Your cargo of treasure now belongs to the pirates. It will be divided among them, but the captain and the quartermaster will get double shares.

COMPENSATION. Pirates look after each other. An injured man will be cared for by his shipmates. He will receive extra pay if he loses a limb.

Handy Hint

Be friendly to the pirate captain. If he likes you, he might treat you like a fellow captain.

I'll never tell you!

FOOD AND DRINK. The pirates will help themselves to your ship's supplies. The food and drink will fill their bellies, not yours.

NO FIGHTING. The captain does not allow fighting on board his ship. Any arguments will be settled by a duel on shore.

NO GAMBLING. The pirate crew is not allowed to bet money on card or dice games on board ship. They must save their gambling for the tavern.

13

Your New Home

The pirates keep you in the ship's hold. You are locked in this dark, rat-infested place day and night. You are ankle-deep in filthy, stinking bilge-water, and stale air fills your lungs. You lose all sense of time. Soon you don't know how long you have been down here.

Forget any thoughts of escape. You cannot climb out of the hold, and even if you could, you wouldn't get very far. The pirates have fitted heavy iron shackles to your legs, so it is very hard for you to move around. You'd better get used to this life!

Your New Shipmates:

QUARTERMASTER. He is the ship's second-in-command. He loves using a cat-o'-nine-tails.

SURGEON. He's quick with a saw, so if you injure a limb he'll have it off in no time.

CARPENTER. He mends the ship's timbers. His skill with a saw means he can do surgeons' work too! That means cutting off a leg!

SAILMAKER. He makes and mends the ship's sails and other canvas items such as covers and awnings.

NAVIGATOR. Using measuring instruments, he plots a safe course for the ship to follow.

COOPER. He makes and repairs the ship's wooden barrels. These hold supplies of food and drink.

ORDINARY SEAMEN. They keep the ship in good order by swabbing the decks, manning the bilge pumps, working the sails, checking the rigging, and so on.

Quartermaster

Carpenter

Surgeon

Navigator

Cooper

Sailmaker

Seaman

In Irons! Shackled to the Deck

A Week of Suffering

When the pirates finally bring you up on deck, it is not because they are feeling sorry for you. Far from it! They are going to try and make you talk. To start, they clamp you in large, heavy leg irons called bilboes. There you stay, fastened to the deck for seven whole days. You feel the full force of nature — the cold wind, the lashing rain, the blistering Sun, and spray from the salty sea. Are you sure you don't want to tell the pirates where the rest of the fleet is?

MONDAY. You are taken from the hold and put in bilboes.

Won't you help me, boy?

TUESDAY. You've had nothing to eat or drink for a day and a night.

WEDNESDAY. You are very thirsty, but you don't drink the salt water you are offered.

THURSDAY. There was a storm last night. The huge waves and movement of the ship make you feel dizzy and seasick.

Your wig

Handy Hint

Lick rainwater from your skin and suck it from your clothes. It's the only freshwater you'll get this week.

FRIDAY. The Sun beats down on your bald head all day, so you get a sunburn.

I can't ! The cap'n would have me flogged!

Bilboes

SATURDAY. You are covered in blisters from the Sun and salty wind, and you are plagued by stinging, biting insects.

SUNDAY. You are thrown back into the hold with the rats and filthy water.

17

Flogged!
Cat-o'-Nine-Tails

THE CAT is nine lengths of rope, each about 2 feet (60 cm) long, tied to a wooden or rope handle. Each of the "tails" has three knots tied in it. The knots are covered in tar to make them hard and sharp.

FISH HOOKS. Some quartermasters are known to tie fish hooks at the end of the cat's tails.

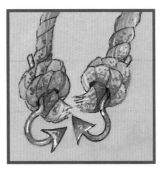

So far, so good. You haven't told the pirates where the rest of the treasure fleet is, so you haven't betrayed your fellow seamen. Now the pirates try to loosen your tongue with a good old-fashioned flogging by the quartermaster with the dreaded cat-o'-nine-tails.

Knots

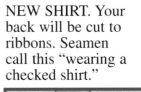

MUSKETBALLS. Some cat-o'-nine-tails have lead musketballs fixed to the tails for extra stinging power.

SALT 'N' VINEGAR. After the flogging, you might have salt and vinegar rubbed into your wounds. It stings!

NEW SHIRT. Your back will be cut to ribbons. Seamen call this "wearing a checked shirt."

As the quartermaster goes to get the cat, you are spreadeagled and tied by your wrists to a grill on deck. The pirate captain decides how many lashes you'll receive. It could be forty, fifty, sixty, or more. At the end of it, he asks you the same questions once again. Will you give in and tell him or not?

Handy Hint

If you're told to make the cat for your own flogging, tie one knot in each tail instead of three.

Groan

Twenty-six...

Vinegar

Salt

Man Overboard!

Water Torture

THE PIRATES have many ingenious ways of using the sea to punish you.

DUCKING. You might be suspended from a yard-arm and ducked into the ocean while the ship sails along. Hold your breath!

TOWING. You might be tied to the end of a rope and tossed into the ocean, then towed along behind the ship for hours.

You are incredibly brave! Despite everything the pirates have done, you haven't told them what they want to know. After the flogging, they keep you in the ship's hold until the cuts on your back have healed. Then they are ready for your next torture.

A rope is passed under the ship, from starboard to port. The pirates tie you to the rope and toss you overboard. You are about to be keelhauled. This means you will be hauled by the rope under the ship's keel. As your back scrapes along the ship's bottom, you will be dragged over the razor-sharp barnacles that grow there. If you don't drown, you might die later from your wounds.

STITCHED UP. You might be sewn into a piece of old sailcloth with other prisoners and thrown overboard.

WEIGHED DOWN. You might be tied to a heavy weight, such as a dead body, and thrown overboard.

TARGET PRACTICE. You might become a target for the pirates to aim at. You'll just have to hope they're bad shots!

Fire! Burning and Barrels

Feel the Heat...

BURNING. Your arms and legs might be tied, and pieces of burning rope might be stuffed between your fingers and toes.

The pirate ship has plenty of gunpowder on board. As you will discover, gunpowder is not just used to shoot cannonballs at other ships.

Once again, the pirates drag you out of the hold. Once again, the captain demands to know where the treasure ships are. When you refuse to tell him, you are grabbed and bundled into a barrel filled with gunpowder. All it takes is one tiny spark to blast the barrel, and you, to smithereens! This could be your last chance to save your skin before you lose it!

MORE THAN A MOUTHFUL. Pieces of oakum (unraveled rope) will be pushed into your mouth and lighted.

BARBECUE. You might be tied to a spit over the ship's cooking fire. You'll be roasted alive!

Diseased and Done For

The gunpowder barrel is the last straw. The thought of being blown to bits is just too much. As the fuse on the gunpowder is about to be lit, you break your silence. When you tell the pirate captain where the rest of the treasure ships are heading, he decides to spare your pathetic life. Actually, he does it to save valuable gunpowder, but he wouldn't tell you that! Now you have to face up to a new danger: disease. You body is in poor condition, and in your weakened state a deadly infection could set in. It would finish you off in no time at all.

I can't take any more!

Symptoms of Sickness:

SCURVY. You will have pale skin, your teeth will fall out and your legs will swell up.

YELLOW FEVER. Mosquitoes carry this horrible disease. You will feel extremely hot for days. Then you'll either get better or vomit black blood and die.

DYSENTERY. This will give you awful pains in the stomach and nonstop diarrhea.

Handy Hint

If you get scurvy, eat lemons, limes, or oranges to make you feel better. (They're full of vitamin C, but you wouldn't know that.)

GANGRENE. If this serious infection sets in to one of your wounds, the surrounding flesh will quickly die. The ship's surgeon (or carpenter) might decide to chop off the infected limb.

Don't worry! It's only a BIT rusty!

Marooned
On a Deserted Island

*T*he pirates have the information they need. You're not worth anything to them now. The last thing they want is for you to catch a deadly disease and pass it on to the rest of the crew. They decide to get rid of you by leaving you stranded and alone on a deserted island. This is called marooning, and you have become a poor, unfortunate marooner. From now on you will have to look after yourself, living off whatever you can find on the island. At least you've seen the last of the pirates! Perhaps, one day, the long arm of the law will catch up with them, and they'll get what they deserve.

CANNIBALS. You hope you won't meet any. You might end up in their cooking pots!

GO MAD. With no one to talk to, you might lose track of time, and you could end up losing your mind.

STARVE. If there is no freshwater or food, it'll be the end of you within a few days.

RESCUE. Keep a lookout for ships on the horizon. Light a fire to let them know you're here and hope they come to your aid.

Handy Hint

If you find footprints in the sand, be careful! Their owner might not be friendly, especially if he's a hungry cannibal!

Now what?!

Saved! The Navy to the Rescue

What Happens to the Pirates?

At last you have some luck! The day after you are marooned, a passing ship sees the smoke from your fire and comes to your rescue. Your saviors are the crew of an English warship of the King's Navy. They were sent to track down the pirates who have been robbing ships.

HUNG BY THE NECK. Captured pirates will be "turned off the cart" — hung until they're dead.

HUNG IN CHAINS. An executed pirate will be bound in iron hoops and left to swing until his bones are picked clean.

HEADS OFF. The heads of executed pirates will be displayed for all to see.

PARDONED. Men forced into piracy and those who have never used weapons against others are pardoned and set free by the court.

Abandon ship!

You give valuable information to the Navy captain, and he easily hunts the pirates down. The pirate sloop is no match for the guns of the warship. The pirate captain and all his crew are taken prisoner. Eventually, you take command of a new ship. You will not get your treasure back, though. The Navy ends up with it!

Handy Hint

Clean yourself up and buy some nice new clothes and a new wig. Get ready to begin life as the captain of a new ship.

Glossary

Avast! A seaman's command to stop doing something.

Barnacle A shelled animal that attaches itself to rocks and wooden objects.

Bilboes A bar with sliding iron shackles fixed to the deck of a ship.

Bilge-water Seawater that collects in the hold of a ship.

Booty Treasure and valuables taken by pirates.

Cannibal An animal that kills and eats its own kind.

Cargo The goods carried in a ship or other vehicle.

Convoy A fleet of vessels that travel together for safety.

Cutlass A heavy sword with a slightly curved blade and a basket-shaped guard to protect the hand.

Flintlock pistol A pistol that fires when a gunflint (a piece of stone) makes a spark that ignites a small charge of gunpowder.

Friction The action of one object rubbing against another.

Galleon A large, slow-moving, heavily armed ship designed to carry cargo.

Haven A place of safety.

Hold The inside of a ship, where cargo is stored.

Jolly Roger The name of the flag flown by a pirate ship. Its name might have come from an old English word "roger," meaning a beggar or the Devil, who was called "Old Roger."

Keel The timber that forms the backbone of a ship.

Musket A gun that fires a ball of lead.

New World A European name for North and South America.

Oakum A substance made from unraveled old rope. It was used to fill cracks in a ship's timbers.

Porcelain A white, hard, shell-like material like pottery, made of clay and rock.

Port The left side of a ship.

Rogue A dishonest or troublesome person.

Scurvy A disease caused by a lack of vitamins in the diet, particularly vitamin C.

Starboard The right side of a ship.

Yard-arm The end of a yard, which was the large beam to which a ship's sails were fixed.

Index